MARGA

COCKTAILS
& PARTY DRINKS

MARGARET FULTON'S BOOK OF
COCKTAILS
& PARTY DRINKS

octopus

CONTENTS

This edition published 1989
by Octopus Illustrated Publishing
Michelin House, 81 Fulham Road
London SW3 6RB
part of Reed International Books

Reprinted 1991, 1992

ISBN 0 7064 5013 2

Produced by Mandarin Offset
Printed and bound in Hong Kong

INTRODUCTION

Cocktails have become extremely popular over the past few years, but they are not a 1980s' invention. The 'cult' of the cocktail dates from the 1920s.

In America, Prohibition banned the production and distribution of strong liquor. No doubt the need to disguise the awful taste of 'boot-leg' spirits which resulted accounted for the enormous variety of drinks enlivened by liqueurs, syrups and fruit juices. By the time Prohibition was repealed in 1933, the fashion for weird and wonderful concoctions was established.

Today cocktail bars are a focal point in most good restaurants, hotels and in many homes.

With the exception of the few classics – such as the Dry Martini – the recipes in this book should not be treated with undue reverence. Try them: if you like them as they are, fine; if they're too dry or too sweet, adapt them to suit your taste. Be adventurous – and try inventing some of your own!

Margaret Fulton

NOTES

Standard spoon and cup measurements are used in all recipes
1 tablespoon = one 20 ml spoon
1 teaspoon = one 5 ml spoon
All spoon measures are level.
Standard cup = 250 ml

A standard measure is called a 'jigger'. It is equivalent to 45 ml/2¼ tablespoons.

For all recipes, quantities are given in both metric and imperial measures. Follow either set but not a mixture of both, because they are not interchangeable.

MIXING COCKTAILS

Fans of James Bond will remember that he always insisted his Dry Martini was shaken, not stirred. Since this holds true for most cocktails, the most basic piece of equipment is a cocktail shaker. It can be any size, shape or material but, for convenience, it should have a built-in strainer. This prevents the ice, whose purpose is only to chill the cocktail, from falling into the glass with the drink. Always shake the shaker vigorously with both hands: this is how you bring the cocktail to life.

Fresh ice must be used for each mixing. Always use large ice cubes for shaking, or serving drinks. Never use small cubes as these dilute the drink too much. Some recipes call for the cocktails to be stirred rather than shaken. This can be done in a tall glass jug or a shaker, using a long-handled spoon. The ice must be strained off before serving.

Teaspoons and tablespoons are needed to measure sugar, cream and certain liquid ingredients. These spoons should be kept in a glass of water when not in use so that they are rinsed between mixes. Nothing spoils the enjoyment of a cocktail more than the slightest hint of something contrary used in the preparation of a different drink.

Certain recipes call for the cocktail to be blended in an electric blender or food processor. If you have a machine with a facility for crushing ice, this presents no problem, but the blades of most machines can be blunted by large ice cubes; therefore you should put only crushed ice into the blending goblet. Ice can be easily crushed by wrapping the cubes in a tea-towel, tying securely and hammering them into smaller pieces with a wooden mallet on a heavy wooden board.

Many recipes call for fruit juice, and freshly squeezed juice is always to be preferred; for this you will need a cone-shaped lemon squeezer. Cartons of fresh orange juice, pineapple juice, etc., are useful for parties. Fruits such as limes are seasonal, so if you have a freezer buy and freeze them when they are in season. All citrus fruits can be stored this way for several months.

Some cocktails call for cream; always use thick cream. Rinse out the shaker thoroughly between mixes as the remains of the cream will adversely affect the flavour of the next mix.

MEASURES

When measuring the ingredients for a cocktail the important thing is to get the proportions right. It doesn't matter what you use for measuring, provided you use the same item for each ingredient; for example, a liqueur glass or egg cup. For this reason I have used the term 'measure' wherever possible. The standard measure is called a 'jigger' and hold 45 ml (2¼ tablespoons). It is well worth buying one of these if you make your own cocktails frequently.

The recipes in this book are for single drinks unless otherwise stated. For two people, double the measure; for three people, triple the measure, and so on.

SERVING COCKTAILS

The cocktail connoisseur demands particular glasses for different drinks. Stocking up with all of the various glasses is expensive, requires a lot of storage space – and is not really necessary. The glasses recommended are limited to five types: the classic V-shaped cocktail glass (preferably the smaller kind, as large cocktails do not stay cold for long); the small tumbler (the kind used to serve whisky); the tall tumbler for longer drinks; the wide Champagne glass for some of the creamy cocktails; and the standard round wine glass. For punches, you can use tumblers, wine glasses, or the cups that usually go with large punch bowls. As cocktails must be served ice-cold, it is perferable to chill the glasses for at least 30 minutes before serving.

Decorations for cocktails range from the stuffed olive and cocktail cherry (now available in other colours besides the traditional red) to slices of fresh fruits, mint sprigs and spices. Always spear cherries on a cocktail stick. Large slices of fruit, such as pineapple or peach, which will not sit well on the edge of a glass, should also be speared on a stick. Never use canned fruit in syrup to decorate, or in the mixing of a cocktail, as the syrup will spoil the flavour.

Suggestions are given for decorations suitable for certain drinks, but experiment with ideas of your own.

STOCKING THE COCKTAIL BAR

Stocking your cocktail bar with all the spirits, liqueurs and syrups needed to mix every kind of cocktail is an expensive business. It is more practical to start off with the basic essentials, involving little more than you would find in the average drinks cabinet, and gradually add to them. If you travel abroad, try the local specialities – if you like them, bring home those items difficult to obtain here.

Grenadine is now quite widely available, but many of the other syrups, such as lemon syrup, are less easy to find. However, the syrups sold for flavouring milk shakes, which are readily available, are perfectly acceptable alternatives.

With the following basic essentials, you will be able to mix most of the drinks in this book: gin, Scotch whisky, vodka, dark rum, white rum, inexpensive brandy, inexpensive Champagne, dry vermouth (French), sweet vermouth (Italian – red), Dubonnet, sherry, Angostura bitters, Cointreau, Curaçao, tequila and grenadine.

To extend your repertoire, add orange bitters, coconut milk, fruit syrups, crème de menthe, Galliano, cherry brandy and Pernod. Gradually increase your selection of liqueurs, whiskies and brandies to make the more unusual cocktails.

GIN COCKTAILS

Gin was originally produced in Holland in the sixteenth century from a distillation of juniper berries, and used as a medicine. In the eighteenth century it acquired a reputation as a rather vulgar drink, but today it is once more considered respectable.

Gin is the most widely used of all spirits for cocktails; it is the basis for all Martini cocktails and the popular Tom Collins. Besides dry gin, there are others – subtly flavoured with fruit. Sloe gin is the best known of these; it is made from the fruit of the wild blackthorn.

Appetizer

1 measure gin
1 measure Dubonnet
juice of ½ orange

Shake the ingredients well with ice and strain into a cocktail glass. Decorate with an orange slice.

Astoria

1 dash of orange bitters
2 measures gin
1 measure dry vermouth

Shake the ingredients well with ice and strain into a cocktail glass.

Caruso

I measure gin
I measure dry vermouth
I measure green crème de menthe

Shake the ingredients well with ice and strain into a cocktail glass. Decorate with a mint sprig if liked.

Fallen Angel

I dash of Angostura bitters
2 dashes of green crème de menthe
juice of I lemon or ½ lime
2 measures gin

Shake the ingredients well with ice and strain into a cocktail glass.

Gimlet

1 measure gin
1 measure lime cordial

Stir the gin and lime cordial together and serve in a
cocktail glass, half-filled with crushed ice if preferred.

Hawaiian

2 measures gin
1 measure orange juice
½ measure orange Curaçao

Shake the ingredients well with ice and strain into a
cocktail glass.

Any orange liqueur may be substituted for Curaçao.

Martini

1 measure gin
1 measure dry vermouth

Shake the ingredients well with ice and strain
into a cocktail glass. Decorate with a stuffed olive
or a twist of lemon peel.

Martini Dry

2 measures gin
1 measure dry vermouth

Shake the ingredients well with ice and strain
into a cocktail glass. Decorate with a stuffed olive
or a twist of lemon peel.

Martini Extra Dry

2 measures gin
1 dash of dry vermouth

Shake the ingredients well with ice and strain
into a cocktail glass. Decorate with a stuffed olive
or a twist of lemon peel.

Martini Sweet

2 measures gin
1 measure sweet vermouth

Shake the ingredients well with ice and strain into a
cocktail glass.

For vodka martinis, simply substitute vodka for gin in any
of these recipes.

Monkey Gland

3 dashes Pernod
3 dashes grenadine
I measure orange juice
2 measures gin

Shake the ingredients well with ice and strain into a
cocktail glass.

One Exciting Night

1 dash of orange juice
1 measure dry vermouth
1 measure sweet vermouth
1 measure gin

Moisten the edge of a port glass or round wine glass
and dip into caster sugar. Shake the ingredients well
with ice and strain into this glass. Decorate with a twist
of lemon peel, if liked.

Tom Collins

juice of ½ lemon
1½ teaspoons caster sugar
2 measures gin
soda water to top up

Shake the ingredients well with ice and strain
into a tall tumbler. Add ice and a good dash of soda water.
Decorate with lemon slices and cocktail cherries.

Silver Streak

1 measure kummel
1 measure gin

Shake the ingredients well with ice and strain into a
cocktail glass.

Kummel is a colourless liqueur, flavoured with caraway.

White Lady

½ measure lemon juice
½ measure Cointreau
1 measure gin

Shake the ingredients well with ice and strain
into a cocktail glass. Decorate with an orange slice,
speared with a cocktail cherry.

Gin Fix

1 tablespoon sugar
juice of ¼ lemon
1 measure water
2 measures gin

Fill a tall tumbler two-thirds full with crushed ice.
Add all the ingredients and stir well. Decorate the rim of
the glass with slices of any fruits in season.

WHISKY COCKTAILS

Contrary to popular belief, the Scots did not invent whisky. The Irish, whose name for it means 'water of life', took it with them, along with the Gaelic language, the kilt and the pipes, when they colonized what later became known as Scotland. Perhaps this is why Irish whiskey is considered more mellow than most blends of Scotch. Canadian whisky and the American bourbon are both corn-based; Scotch comes from malted cereals.

A selection of different whiskies is ideal, but not essential. Scotch can be used in place of bourbon, Canadian or Irish whiskey in cocktails calling for these spirits, although the taste will not be quite the same.

Bobby Burns

1 measure sweet vermouth
1 measure Scotch whisky
3 dashes of Benedictine

Shake the ingredients well with ice and strain into a cocktail glass. Decorate with a twist of lemon peel.

This is one of the best of the whisky cocktails, as befits a drink named in honour of Scotland's greatest poet.

Brainstorm

1 measure Irish whiskey
2 dashes of Benedictine
2 dashes of dry vermouth

Stir the ingredients together with ice in a shaker or jug and strain into a cocktail glass. Decorate with a twist of orange peel.

Rusty Nail

1 measure Scotch whisky
1 measure Drambuie

Pour the whisky onto ice cubes in a whisky tumbler.
Float the Drambuie on top by pouring it over the back of
a teaspoon onto the whisky.

Cowboy

2 measures whisky
1 measure thick cream

Shake the ingredients together vigorously with cracked ice
and strain into a cocktail glass.

Rattlesnake

8 measures Canadian whisky
2 egg whites
2 measures lemon juice
a little sugar
5 dashes Pernod

Shake the ingredients together vigorously with ice and
strain though a fine sieve into cocktail glasses.
6 servings

Be careful with this drink. It is said to cure the bite, kill the
snake or bring it out of the woodwork!

23

Manhattan

I dash of Angostura bitters
2 measures Canadian whisky
I measure sweet vermouth

Shake the ingredients well with ice and strain
into a cocktail glass.

Manhattan Dry

½ measure dry vermouth
½ measure sweet vermouth
I measure Canadian whisky

Stir the ingredients together with ice in a shaker or jug.
Strain into a cocktail glass.

Manhattan Sweet

I measure sweet vermouth
I measure Canadian whisky

Stir the ingredients well with ice in a shaker or jug
and strain into a cocktail glass.

Whisky Sour

juice of ½ lemon
I ½ teaspoons sugar
2 measures whisky
soda water to top up

Shake the ingredients well with ice and strain
into a small tumbler. Add a good dash of soda water.
Decorate with a slice of orange and a cocktail cherry.

Old-Fashioned Cocktail

1 sugar lump
2 dashes of Angostura bitters
2 measures Canadian whisky

Soak the sugar lump with the bitters in a small tumbler.
Crush the sugar with the back of a spoon. Add a
lump of ice, a twist of lemon peel and a slice of orange.
Pour on the whisky and stir well.

Variations of this cocktail can be made by substituting
brandy, gin, rum, vodka, etc. for the whisky.

Cup Final

I measure Scotch whisky
I measure dry vermouth
I measure pineapple juice

Shake the ingredients well with ice and strain
into a cocktail glass. Decorate with a pineapple slice and
a cocktail cherry.

Not just for one night of the year, but after every game,
either as a celebration or a consolation!

Whisky Highball

2 measures whisky
soda water to top up

Place a lump of ice in a tumbler and add the whisky.
Top up with soda water. Decorate with a twist of lemon
peel.

Ginger ale can be used in place of soda water.

Earthquake

1 measure gin
1 measure whisky
1 measure Pernod

Shake the ingredients well with ice and strain into a
cocktail glass.

This cocktail means what it says, and more than one
should not be offered to the inexperienced!

Whisky Fix

2 teaspoons caster sugar
1 teaspoon water
juice of ½ lemon
2 measures Bourbon whiskey

Dissolve the sugar in the water in a tumbler and fill the
glass two-thirds full with crushed ice. Add the remaining
ingredients and stir well. Decorate the rim of the glass
with slices of fruits in season.

BRANDY COCKTAILS

There are almost as many brandies on the market as there are cocktails. Some, such as the finest Cognacs and Armagnacs, are too fine and too expensive for use in cocktails. For the novice cocktail mixer, the wisest course is to select a three-star brandy; local brandies are excellent.

The fruit brandies, such as Calvados (apple), kirsch (cherry), apricot and peach, are not really brandies but liqueurs; however, they often blend well with brandy in a cocktail.

Brandy Fix

1 teaspoon sugar
1 teaspoon water
juice of ½ lemon
½ measure cherry brandy
1 measure brandy

Dissolve the sugar in the water in a tumbler.
Add the remaining ingredients and fill with crushed ice.
Stir, place a lemon slice in the drink and serve with a straw.

Brandy Egg Sour

1 egg
1 teaspoon caster sugar
3 dashes of lemon juice
1 measure orange Curaçao
1 measure brandy

Shake the ingredients well with ice and strain
into a tumbler. Decorate with an orange slice speared on a
cocktail stick with a cherry. Serve with straws.

Angel Face

1 measure gin
1 measure apricot brandy
1 measure Calvados

Shake the ingredients well with ice and strain into a
cocktail glass.

Corpse Reviver

½ measure sweet vermouth
½ measure Calvados
1 measure brandy

Shake the ingredients well with ice and strain into a
cocktail glass.

Stinger

¼ measure white crème de menthe
¾ measure brandy

Shake the ingredients well with ice and strain into a
cocktail glass.

Brandy Alexander

1 measure brandy
½ measure crème de cacao
1 measure thick cream
little grated nutmeg

Shake the ingredients well with ice and strain into a wide
champagne glass. Sprinkle with grated nutmeg.

Between-the-Sheets

1 dash of lemon juice
1 measure brandy
1 measure Cointreau
1 measure dark rum

Shake the ingredients well with ice and strain into a
cocktail glass.

Widow's Kiss

1 dash of Angostura bitters
½ measure Chartreuse
½ measure Benedictine
1 measure Calvados

Shake the ingredients well with ice and strain into a
cocktail glass.

Paradise

1 dash of lemon juice
½ measure orange juice
1 measure gin
½ measure apricot brandy

Shake the ingredients well with ice and strain into a
cocktail glass. Decorate with orange and lemon slices.

Sidecar

½ measure lemon juice
½ measure Cointreau
1 measure brandy

Shake the ingredients well with ice and strain into a
cocktail glass, half-filled with crushed ice if perferred.
Decorate with a twist of lemon.

Baltimore Egg Nogg

1 egg
1 1/2 teaspoons sugar
1/2 measure brandy
1/2 measure dark rum
1/2 measure Madeira or sherry
1 1/4 cups milk
little grated nutmeg

Shake the ingredients well with ice and strain into a tall tumbler. Sprinkle a little grated nutmeg on top.

Egg Nogg

1 egg
1 tablespoon caster sugar
2 measures brandy
2 measures milk
little grated nutmeg

Shake the ingredients well with ice and strain into a tall tumbler. Sprinkle a little grated nutmeg on top.

Brandy Flip

1 egg
1 1/2 teaspoons caster sugar
2 measures brandy
little grated nutmeg

Shake the ingredients well with ice and strain into a tumbler. Sprinkle a little grated nutmeg on top.

For a creamier version, blend the ingredients in an electric blender. Port, rum, sherry or whisky can be used in place of brandy.

VODKA COCKTAILS

Both the Poles and the Russians claim the glory of inventing vodka. For our purposes, vodkas produced in either of these countries, being expensive imports, are wasted in mixing cocktails. They are best drunk neat, accompanied by caviar or salted fish. Vodka produced locally, with a milder and less distinctive taste, is more suitable for mixing with other ingredients. Incidentally, the Bloody Mary, as well as being a fine drink for the evening, is a great pick-me-up first thing in the morning. The Harvey Wallbanger is perhaps the most popular vodka-based cocktail.

Bloody Mary

1 measure vodka
2 measures tomato juice
⅓ measure lemon juice
1 dash of Worcestershire sauce
salt and pepper to taste

Shake the ingredients well with ice and strain into a wine glass. Garnish with celery leaves.

Black Russian

2 measures vodka
1 measure Kahlua

Pour the vodka and Kahlua over ice cubes in a whisky tumbler.

For a white Russian, top up with thick cream. For a longer drink, use a tall tumbler and top up with coca-cola.

Harvey Wallbanger

1 measure vodka
4 measures orange juice
½ measure Galliano

Pour the vodka and orange juice over ice cubes
in a tall tumbler and stir well. Float the Galliano on top
by pouring it over the back of a teaspoon onto the
vodka and orange.

Moscow Mule

juice of ½ lime
large twist of lime peel
1 ½ measures vodka
ginger beer to top up

Pour the lime juice into a tall tumbler and
drop in the twist of peel. Add ice cubes and pour in the
vodka. Top up with ginger beer. Stir and decorate with
lime slices.

Screwdriver

2 measures vodka
orange juice to top up

Pour the vodka over ice cubes in a tumbler
and top up with orange juice. Stir well and decorate
with orange slices.

Vodka Martini

1 measure vodka
1 measure dry vermouth

Shake the ingredients well with ice and strain
into a cocktail glass. Decorate with a twist of lemon.

For other Vodka Martinis see Gin Martinis (page 14).

Vodka Gimlet

1 measure lime juice
1 ½ measures vodka
1 teaspoon caster sugar

Shake the ingredients well with ice and strain
into a cocktail glass. Decorate with a lemon or lime slice.

Vodka Collins

juice of 1 lime
1 teaspoon caster sugar
2 measures vodka
soda water to top up

Shake the ingredients well with ice and strain into
a tall tumbler. Add ice and top up with soda water.
Decorate with lemon and lime slices, and a cherry.

RUM COCKTAILS

Rum will be forever associated with the West Indies, its true home, and the Royal Navy, its second home. Rum comes in various colours and strengths – and the strong versions are pretty powerful. White rum, which is colourless, was originally known as Cuban rum.

Locally made rum is an excellent base for cocktails because its flavour blends particularly well with fruit juices and other spirits. It is the base for one of the great cocktails, the Daiquiri.

Light Rum Cocktail

½ measure lemon or lime juice
½ measure grenadine
I measure white rum

Shake the ingredients well with ice and strain into a cocktail glass.

Rum Special

I teaspoon grenadine
I measure gin
2 measures white rum
juice of ½ lime

Shake the ingredients well with ice and strain into a cocktail glass.

Santa Cruz Fix

1 teaspoon sugar
1 teaspoon water
juice of ½ lemon
½ measure cherry brandy
1 measure dark rum

Dissolve the sugar in the water in a tumbler,
add the remaining ingredients and fill with crushed ice. Stir
slowly, then add a slice of lemon and serve with a straw.

Zombie

1 measure dark rum
1 measure white rum
1 measure pineapple juice
1 teaspoon caster sugar

Shake the ingredients well with ice and strain
into a tall tumbler. Decorate with a cocktail cherry and
pineapple slices.

47

Daiquiri

juice of ¼ lemon or ½ lime
1 teaspoon caster sugar
2 measures dark or white rum

Shake the ingredients well with ice and strain into a
cocktail glass. Decorate with a cocktail cherry.

Little Devil

½ measure lemon juice
½ measure Cointreau
1 measure dark rum
1 measure gin

Shake the ingredients well with ice and strain into a
cocktail glass.

Pina Colada

2 measures dark rum
3 tablespoons coconut milk
2 tablespoons crushed pineapple

Place the ingredients in an electric blender. Add two cups
of crushed ice and blend at high speed for 30 seconds.
Strain into a tall tumbler and serve with a straw.

Parisian Blonde

1 measure thick cream
little caster sugar
1 measure orange Curaçao
1 measure dark rum

Shake the ingredients well with ice and strain into a
cocktail glass. Decorate with orange slices.

Cuba Libre

2 measures dark rum
juice of ½ lime
coca-cola to top up

Half-fill a tall tumbler with ice cubes.
Add the rum and lime juice and stir well.
Top up with coca-cola and decorate with lime slices.

Rum Collins

juice of 1 lime
1 teaspoon caster sugar
2 measures dark rum
soda water to top up

Shake the ingredients well with ice and strain
into a tall tumbler. Add ice cubes, top up with
soda water and stir well. Decorate with a slice of lemon
and a cocktail cherry. Serve with a straw.

TEQUILA COCKTAILS

Tequila is a Mexican spirit, distilled from pulque which, in turn, is distilled from the sap of the maguey plant, a vegetable similar to a cactus. Tequila is a refined form of mescal, taken by the Indians of Mexico as part of their religious ceremonies.

All recipes for tequila cocktails are modern, as this spirit has only recently acquired a respectable reputation in society, being pioneered chiefly in southern California. Salt is used in the Margarita, since tequila is traditionally drunk as a neat spirit with just salt and lemon juice on the tongue.

Corcovado

1 measure blue Curaçao
1 measure tequila
1 measure Drambuie
lemonade to top up

Shake the ingredients well with ice and strain into
a tall tumbler filled with crushed ice. Top up with
lemonade and decorate with a slice of lemon or lime.
Serve with a straw.

Margarita

1 ½ measures tequila
½ measure Cointreau
1 measure lemon or lime juice

Moisten the inner and outer edge of a cocktail glass
with a slice of lemon or lime and dip in fine salt.
Shake the ingredients well with ice and strain into the glass.

Tequila Sunrise

1 ¾ measures tequila
3 ½ measures orange juice
½ measure grenadine

Stir the tequila and orange juice with
ice cubes in a shaker or jug and strain into
a tall tumbler. Add ice cubes then slowly pour in the
grenadine. Allow to settle, but stir once before drinking.

Viva Maria

1 measure tequila
½ measure lime juice
¼ measure maraschino
½ teaspoon grenadine
½ egg white

Shake the ingredients well with ice and strain
into a wide champagne glass half-filled with crushed ice.
Decorate with a lemon slice, a lime slice
and a cocktail cherry.

CHAMPAGNE COCKTAILS

Some prefer Champagne at breakfast time, in or out of cocktails; the classic Champagne cocktail – Buck's Fizz (page 60) is traditionally enjoyed at this hour. Others feel that the effervescence of this wine, which epitomizes the lively spirit of the 1920s, is more suitable at night. The important thing to remember is that it is not necessary to spend a lot of money on Champagne for cocktails – inexpensive Champagne, or even sparkling white wine, is very good.

Never put Champagne in an electric blender or food processor – you may end up with your cocktail on the walls!

Basic Champagne Cocktail

1 sugar lump
few dashes of Angostura bitters
Champagne to top up

Place a lump of sugar in a wine glass
and saturate it with Angostura bitters. Add a lump of ice
and top up with Champagne. Add a twist of lemon peel
and decorate with an orange slice.

New Orleans Dandy

1 measure light rum
½ measure peach brandy
1 dash of orange juice
1 dash of lime juice
Champagne to top up

Shake the ingredients well with ice and strain
into a large wine glass. Top up with Champagne and
decorate with an orange slice and a cocktail cherry.

California Dreaming

2 dashes of kirsch
3 measures pineapple juice
1 dash of lemon juice
Champagne to top up

Put the ingredients in an electric blender with a few ice cubes and blend for 30 seconds. Pour into a wine glass and top up with Champagne. Decorate with pineapple.

Americana

1 measure Bourbon whiskey
½ teaspoon caster sugar
1 dash of Angostura bitters
Champagne to top up

Stir the ingredients in a wide Champagne glass until the sugar has dissolved. Top up with Champagne and decorate with a peach slice on a cocktail stick.

Honeydew

1 measure gin
½ measure lemon juice
1 dash of Pernod
60 g (2 oz) Honeydew melon, diced
Champagne to top up

Place the ingredients, with some ice cubes,
in an electric blender. Blend for 30 seconds, then pour into
a large wine glass. Top up with Champagne and decorate
with small pieces of melon.

Paddy's Night

1 measure green crème de menthe
1 measure Irish whiskey
Champagne to top up

Shake the ingredients well with ice and strain into a large
wine glass. Top up with Champagne to serve.

FIZZES & SLINGS

Fizzes and Slings are long, gently sparkling drinks, ideal for warm summer evenings. The names of the Sling recipes reflect their popularity among the administrators and plantation owners of the British Empire in the Far East in the 1920s and 1930s: theirs was the world intimately described in the short stories of Somerset Maugham. Fizzes have always been popular in the USA, especially in the southern States. Both Slings and Fizzes are ideal types of cocktails for the drinker who wants to experiment. Remember, too, that a couple of the fruity ones a day will provide you with all the vitamin C you need!

Gin Sling

1 teaspoon sugar
2 measures gin
mineral or soda water to top up

Dissolve the sugar in a little water in a tall tumbler. Add the gin and a lump of ice. Top up with mineral water or soda water. Serve with straws.

Buck's Fizz

½ cup orange juice
(approximately)
Champagne to top up

Fill a tall tumbler with crushed ice. Fill a quarter of the glass with orange juice and top up with Champagne. Decorate with an orange slice.

Dubonnet Fizz

juice of ½ orange
juice of ¼ lemon
I teaspoon cherry brandy
2 measures Dubonnet
soda water to top up

Shake the ingredients well with ice, strain into a
tumbler and fill with soda water. Decorate with fruit.

Imperial Fizz

juice of ½ lemon
I measure dark rum
2 measures Canadian whisky
I ½ teaspoons caster sugar
soda water to top up

Shake the ingredients well with ice, strain into a tumbler
and fill with soda water.

Silver Fizz

juice of ½ lemon
1 ½ teaspoons caster sugar
2 measures gin
1 egg white
soda water to top up

Shake the ingredients well, strain into a tall tumbler and fill
with soda water. Add a twist of lemon peel.
For a Golden Fizz, replace the egg white with a yolk.

Pineapple Fizz

2 tablespoons pineapple juice
1 ½ teaspoons caster sugar
2 measures dark rum
soda water to top up

Shake the ingredients well with ice, strain into a tall tumbler
and fill with soda water. Decorate with pineapple.

Strawberry Blush

juice of ½ lemon or 1 lime
4 strawberries, crushed
1 ½ teaspoons caster sugar
1 tablespoon thick cream
2 measures gin
soda water to top up

Shake the ingredients well with ice, strain into a tall
tumbler and fill with soda water. Decorate with
strawberry slices.

Orange Fizz

juice of ½ orange
juice of ¼ lemon or ½ lime
2 measures gin
soda water to top up

Shake the ingredients well with ice, strain into
a tall tumbler and fill with soda water. Decorate with
orange and lime slices.

Ruby Fizz

juice of ½ lemon
1 teaspoon caster sugar
1 egg white
2 dashes of raspberry syrup
or grenadine
2 measures sloe gin
soda water to top up

Shake the ingredients well with ice, strain into a tall tumbler
and fill with soda water.

Brandy Fizz

juice of ½ lemon
1 ½ teaspoons caster sugar
2 measures brandy
soda water to top up

Shake the ingredients well with ice, strain into a tall tumbler and fill with soda water. Decorate with a lemon slice.

Derby

5 dashes of lemon juice
1 teaspoon caster sugar
1 egg
2 measures Canadian whisky
3 dashes of orange Curaçao
soda water to top up

Shake the ingredients well with ice, strain into a tumbler and fill with soda water.

Cream Fizz

juice of ½ lemon
1½ teaspoons caster sugar
2 measures gin
1 teaspoon thick cream
soda water to top up

Shake the ingredients well with ice, strain into
a tall tumbler and fill with soda water.

Morning Glory

juice of ½ lemon or 1 lime
1½ teaspoons caster sugar
1 egg white
2 dashes of Pernod
2 measures whisky
soda water to top up

Shake the ingredients well with ice, stain into a tall tumbler
and fill with soda water. Decorate with lime slices.

Singapore Sling

juice of ¼ lemon
½ measure gin
1 measure cherry brandy
soda water to top up

Shake the ingredients well with ice and strain
into a tall tumbler. Top up with soda water and add a
lump of ice. Decorate with cocktail cherries and
a lemon slice. Serve with straws.

Straits Sling

8 measures gin
2 measures Benedictine
2 measures cherry brandy
juice of 2 lemons
1 teaspoon Angostura bitters
1 teaspoon orange bitters
soda water to top up

Shake the ingredients well with ice and strain
into tall tumblers. Top up with soda water. Decorate with
orange and lemon slices. Serve with straws.
6 servings

WINE CUPS AND PUNCHES

With wine cups and punches, it is a waste of money to use costly wines. The subtleties of ten-year-old Claret when mixed with fruit juices, sugar and liqueurs are lost to all of us. In recipes calling for Claret, use a light crisp flagon or cask red. When the recipe calls for white wine don't use a precious bottle from your cellar. Excellent cask wine is available. Rhine Riesling, Sauterne and Moselle are all delicious but be sure they are well chilled before adding to the bowl.

You can flavour your punch with slices of any fruit you like: e.g., orange, lemon, lime, apple, pineapple, banana, strawberry, raspberry, pear, peach, plum or apricot.

Champagne Cup

1 tablespoon caster sugar
2 measures brandy
2 measures orange Curaçao
1 measure maraschino
1 measure Grand Marnier
1.2 litres (5 cups) Champagne, chilled

Put the ingredients into a large bowl. Add ice and stir well. Decorate with orange and pineapple slices.
4 to 6 servings

Cider Cup

1 measure maraschino
1 measure orange Curaçao
1 measure brandy
1.2 litres (5 cups) medium dry cider, chilled

Pour the ingredients into a large glass jug or bowl. Add ice and stir gently. Decorate with fruits in season.
4 to 6 servings

Claret Cup

1 measure maraschino
2 measures orange Curaçao
2 tablespoons caster sugar
1.2 litres (5 cups) Claret

Put the ingredients into a large bowl. Add ice and stir until the sugar is dissolved. Decorate with fruits in season.
4 to 6 servings

Peach Cup

2 ripe peaches
1.5 litres (6 cups) still Moselle, chilled
3 tablespoons caster sugar
750 ml (3 cups) sparkling Moselle, chilled

Peel and chop the peaches into a large bowl. Pour half of the still Moselle over the fruit. Add the sugar, stir gently, then cover and leave for 30 minutes. Add the remaining still Moselle.
Just before serving, add the sparkling Moselle.
8 to 10 servings

This cup must be served chilled but no ice should be placed in the drink.

Rhine Wine Cup

2 measures maraschino
1 measure orange Curaçao
1 ½ teaspoons caster sugar
1.2 litres (5 cups) medium white wine

Place the ingredients in a large jug or bowl. Add a few pieces of ice and stir well. Decorate with fruits in season.
4 to 6 servings

Brandy Punch

juice of 15 lemons
juice of 4 oranges
3 cups caster sugar
1¼ cups orange Curaçao
2 measures grenadine
2.25 litres (10 cups) brandy
2.25 litres (10 cups) sparkling mineral water

Pour the fruit juices into a jug. Add the sugar and stir until dissolved. Place a large quantity of ice in a large punch bowl, add all the ingredients and stir well. Decorate with lemon and orange slices.
15 to 20 servings

Cardinal Punch

2½ cups caster sugar
2.25 litres (10 cups) sparkling mineral water
2.25 litres (10 cups) Claret
2½ cups brandy
2½ cups rum
2½ cups sparkling white wine
2 measures Italian vermouth

Dissolve the sugar in the mineral water, then pour into a
large punch bowl containing a large quantity of ice. Add
the remaining ingredients and stir gently. Keep the punch
bowl packed with ice.
25 to 30 servings

Bombay Punch

1.2 litres (5 cups) brandy
1.2 litres (5 cups) sherry
⅔ cup maraschino
⅔ cup orange Curaçao
4.5 litres (20 cups) Champagne
2.25 litres (10 cups) sparkling mineral water

Pour the ingredients into a large punch bowl containing plenty of ice cubes and stir gently. Decorate with fruits in season. Keep the punch bowl packed with ice.
30 to 35 servings

Champagne Punch

1 ¼ cups caster sugar
2.25 litres (10 cups) Champagne
1.2 litres (5 cups) sparkling mineral water
2 measures brandy
2 measures maraschino
2 measures orange Curaçao

Put the ingredients into a large punch bowl containing plenty of ice cubes and stir until the sugar is dissolved. Add slices of fruits in season.
15 to 20 servings

Roman Punch

5 cups caster sugar
juice of 3 oranges
juice of 10 lemons
1.2 litres (5 cups) Champagne
1.2 litres (5 cups) dark rum
½ measure orange bitters
grated rind of 1 orange
10 egg whites, beaten

Dissolve the sugar in the fruit juices in a large punch bowl.
Add the Champagne, rum, orange bitters, orange rind and
the egg whites. Add plenty of ice cubes and stir well. Keep
the bowl packed with ice. Decorate with orange slices.
15 to 20 servings

Fish House Punch

1 ¼ cups caster sugar
juice of 6 lemons
1 ¼ cups brandy
⅔ cup peach brandy
⅔ cup dark rum
1.75 litres (7½ cups) sparkling mineral water

Dissolve the sugar in the lemon juice in a jug, then transfer to a large punch bowl containing plenty of ice. Add all of the remaining ingredients and stir gently. Decorate with lemon slices.
12 to 15 servings

Claret Punch

1 ¼ cups caster sugar
3.5 litres (15 cups) Claret
2.25 litres (10 cups) sparkling mineral water
1 ¼ cups lemon juice
2 measures orange Curaçao

Place the ingredients in a large punch bowl containing
plenty of ice. Stir gently until the sugar is dissolved.
Decorate with slices of fruits in season. Keep the punch
bowl packed with ice.
20 to 25 servings

Sauterne Punch

1 ¼ cups caster sugar
2.25 litres (10 cups) Sauterne
1 measure maraschino
1 measure orange Curaçao
1 measure Grand Marnier

Dissolve the sugar in the wine in a large jug, then pour
over a large quantity of ice in a punch bowl and stir in the
remaining ingredients. Add slices of fruits in season.
10 to 15 servings

Any other medium sweet white wine can be used in
place of Sauterne.

NON-ALCOHOLIC COCKTAILS

When giving a cocktail party it is only polite to offer something interesting to drink to those guests who don't want to drink alcohol. With the all year round availability of fruit juices, the range of syrups for sale and a little creativity on your part, this presents an ideal opportunity for experimenting. A colourful and gaily decorated 'mocktail' is indistinguishable on sight from its 'weightier' counterparts.

Non-alcoholic cocktails are, of course, delicious alternatives to less exciting cold drinks at any time of the day. They are also perfect for children.

Appleade

2 large eating apples
2½ cups boiling water
½ teaspoon sugar

Chop the apples and place in a bowl. Pour the boiling water over the apples and add the sugar. Leave to stand for 10 minutes, then strain into a jug and allow to cool. Pour over ice cubes in a tall tumbler and decorate with an apple slice. Serve with a straw.

3 servings

Anita

1 measure orange juice
1 measure lemon juice
3 dashes of Angostura bitters
soda water to top up

Shake the ingredients well with ice. Strain into a tumbler and top up with soda water. Decorate with lemon and orange slices. Serve with a straw.

Cinderella

1 measure lemon juice
1 measure pineapple juice
1 measure orange juice
1 dash of grenadine
soda water to top up

Shake the ingredients well with ice and strain into a tall tumbler. Top up with soda water and decorate with pineapple slices. Serve with a straw.

Clayton's Pussyfoot

½ measure lemon syrup
½ measure orange juice
1 measure coca-cola

Shake the ingredients well with ice and strain into a cocktail glass.

Jersey Lily

1 wine glass sparkling apple juice
2 dashes of Angostura bitters
¼ teaspoon caster sugar

Stir the ingredients with ice in a jug or shaker, then strain into a wine glass. Decorate with a cocktail cherry.

Nursery Fizz

4 tablespoons orange juice
(approximately)
4 tablespoons ginger ale
(approximately)

Fill a large wine glass with crushed ice and pour in equal measures of orange juice and ginger ale. Decorate with a cocktail cherry and an orange slice speared onto a cocktail stick. Serve with a straw.

Carib Cream

I small banana, chopped
I measure lemon juice
I measure milk
I teaspoon finely chopped walnuts

Place the banana, lemon juice and milk in an electric
blender with some crushed ice and blend on maximum
speed until smooth. Pour into a cocktail glass and sprinkle
the chopped walnuts on top just before serving.

Café Astoria

I teaspoon instant coffee powder or
½ measure coffee essence
2 measures milk
¼ measure pineapple juice
¼ measure lemon juice
chocolate flakes to decorate

Place the ingredients in an electric blender with some
crushed ice and blend on maximum speed for 30 seconds.
Pour into a cocktail glass and sprinkle chocolate flakes on
top just before serving.

Temperance Mocktail

2 measures lemon juice
2 dashes of grenadine
I egg yolk

Shake the ingredients well with ice and strain into a
cocktail glass. Decorate with a cocktail cherry.

San Francisco

1 measure orange juice
1 measure lemon juice
1 measure pineapple juice
1 measure grapefruit juice
2 dashes of grenadine
1 egg white
soda water to top up

Shake the ingredients well with ice and strain into a wine glass. Top up with soda water and decorate with fruit slices speared onto a cocktail stick. Serve with a straw.

Tenderberry

6-8 strawberries
I measure grenadine
I measure thick cream
I measure dry ginger ale
little ground ginger

Place the strawberries, grenadine and cream in an electric
blender with some crushed ice and blend on maximum
speed for 30 seconds. Pour into a tumbler. Add the dry
ginger and stir. Sprinkle a little ginger on top and decorate
with a strawberry, if liked.

Parson's Special

4 dashes of grenadine
½ cup orange juice
1 egg yolk

Shake the ingredients well with ice and strain into a tumbler.

Keep Sober

½ measure grenadine
½ measure lemon syrup
3 measures tonic water
soda water to top up

Stir the ingredients together in a tumbler. Top up with soda water. Add ice cubes if liked.

Limey

1 measure lime juice
½ measure lemon juice
½ egg white

Shake the ingredients well with ice and strain into a cocktail glass. Decorate with a cocktail cherry.

St. Clements

2 measures orange juice
2 measures bitter lemon

Stir the ingredients well with ice in a shaker or jug and strain into a tall tumbler. Add ice cubes and decorate with orange and lemon slices. Serve with a straw.

Warbine Cooler

2 dashes Angostura bitters
1 dash lime juice
ginger beer to top up

Stir the bitters and lime juice together in a large wine glass.
Top up with ginger beer and decorate with lime slices.
Serve with a straw.

Apple Eye

2 measures apple juice
½ measure blackcurrant juice
1 measure thick cream
little ground cinnamon

Place the apple juice, blackcurrant juice and cream in an
electric blender with some crushed ice. Blend on
maximum speed for 30 seconds. Pour into a cocktail glass
and sprinkle a little cinnamon on top. Decorate with apple
slices.

Sweet 'n' Sour

2 measures lime cordial
1 ½ measures thick cream
1 teaspoon honey
3 dashes of Angostura bitters

Place the lime cordial, cream and honey in an electric
blender with some crushed ice and blend until smooth.
Pour into a cocktail glass and add the Angostura bitters.
Stir and serve.

INDEX

Acknowledgments

Recipes by Joe Turner
Photography by Paul Williams
Photographic stylist: Penny Markham